Barry Fantoni, novelist, broadcaster, jazz musician, reviewer, illustrator, film and TV actor, *Private Eye* contributor, *The Times* diary cartoonist, was born on February 28, 1940.

Barry Fantoni's Chinese Horoscopes

THE GOAT

SPHERE BOOKS LIMITED

SPHERE BOOKS LIMITED

Penguin Books Ltd, 27 Wrights Lane, London W8 5TZ (Publishing and Editorial) *and* Harmondsworth, Middlesex, England (Distribution and Warehouse)
Viking Penguin Inc., 40 West 23rd Street, New York, New York 10010, USA
Penguin Books Australia Ltd, Ringwood, Victoria, Australia
Penguin Books Canada Ltd, 2801 John Street, Markham, Ontario, Canada L3R 1B4
Penguin Books (NZ) Ltd, 182–190 Wairau Road, Auckland 10, New Zealand

First published in Great Britain by Sphere Books Ltd 1987

Made and printed in Great Britain by
Richard Clay Ltd, Bungay, Suffolk
Filmset in $9\frac{1}{2}$/10pt Photina

To my family of Roosters

Acknowledgements

I should like to express my thanks to all those many friends, relatives and strangers who have both knowingly and otherwise helped with the compilation of this book. I should like to thank in particular Gillian Jason who researched the beautiful Chinese illustrations, The British Library for granting permission to reproduce them, and Dr Hin Hung Ho for the delightful calligraphy. But the bulk of my gratitude is reserved for my Rooster wife who ploughed on relentlessly with the list of celebrities whose names are scattered throughout, and without which this book could never have been written.

Introduction

How do you introduce yourself? Do you first give your name, or say what school you went to, or where you live, or what kind of job you do? Whatever you say, the chances are that you will be attempting in some small way to summarise who you imagine yourself to be, and hoping that the label you choose will do the *real* you justice.

In the East, however, introductions may take on a very different form. Because of a system that has evolved throughout Eastern civilisation, everyone has a birth sign named after one of the twelve animals that make up the Chinese Horoscope. Consequently, when two strangers meet, instead of giving their names, they might well refer to their animal sign. 'I am a Goat,' one might say.

'Pleased to meet you,' might come the reply, 'I am a Pig.'

As a result of this simple greeting, a great deal of unspoken information will have changed hands. In that particular case, if they had met to discuss business, both Goat and Pig will probably have parted on good terms. However, if the Pig had been a Rooster I suspect that the two Chinese businessmen would have given the meeting a miss. And for a very good reason. For the Peoples of the East, an individual's personal animal sign, dictated by the year of birth, plays a central role in the conduct of their daily lives. Since I was introduced to the system some thirteen years ago, it has revolutionised mine. Chinese horoscopes have shown me a completely fresh way of viewing human behaviour, one that can be of great practical use. It can, for example, guide us to the best business associate, help us in our choice of marriage partners and even suggest the ideal lover. Chinese Horoscopes tell us why we dress like we do, why some of us save every penny while others spend without caring. We learn why some are content to sit at home while others travel to the four corners of the globe. It explains who we really are, not only to the world at large, but more importantly to ourselves.

No one is certain how the Chinese Horoscope first came into being, but there is, as with all mysteries, a legend which I believe makes up in poetical charm what it lacks in scientific probability.

Five centuries before the birth of Christ, so the legend has it, the Buddha sent out an invitation to all the animals in his Kingdom, asking if they would join him in the New Year celebrations. For reasons that seem only known to the animals themselves, only twelve turned up. In order of arrival there came: the rat, the buffalo, the tiger, the cat, the dragon, the snake, the horse, the goat, the monkey, the rooster, the dog and last of all the pig. Cheered by their presence, the Buddha decided to show his gratitude by honouring each animal with a year, calling it by their name. Moreover, all people born in that year would inherit the animal's characteristics. Goats would be charming and artistic, Dogs would be anxious and loyal. Unlike Western astrology which is based on the movement of the sun and the stars, the Chinese use the lunar cycle. There are twelve moons in a lunar cycle, plus an extra moon every thirteen (our Blue Moon), which is why the Chinese New Year never falls on the same day. So, with twelve moons and twelve animals there evolved a perfect pattern. Heaven alone knows what would have happened if a few camels and ducks had decided to show up for the Buddha's party!

Given such an explanation, the most obvious question for us Western sceptics to ask is how on earth can all those born in the same year inherit the same characteristics? The answer is of course that we are not all identical. And it was only when I had stopped asking that same question about the thousands of people I didn't know, asking instead if it were true of myself, that I discovered that the system of Chinese Horoscopes really worked. Testing the system first on my own sign, then on my family and friends, and finally on a large number of celebrities whose lives I am familiar with, I was left in no doubt that it was startlingly accurate. In other words, instead of generalising, I looked at specific cases. And once I had shed my scepticism I began to understand more clearly the Chinese view of the twelve animal signs, and the influence they exercise over our lives.

The sign of our parents, the sign of marriage and business partners and the signs of our children all create variations on the way our own animal sign influences us. The eager to please Dragon son will benefit enormously from his adoring Rooster mother, while the passionate Rat will find the anxious Dog impervious to her advances. Time of birth is another factor which determines a subtle difference in temperament. Goats born in the summer will be less capricious than those born in winter, whereas Snakes born during a sudden thunderstorm will be in danger all their lives.

This book gives an idea of the markedly different attitudes between the two cultures of East and West. To seek pleasure and enjoyment from life is an inherent part of Chinese philosophy. The West on the other hand, frowns on those who treat life like a game. The East recognises that the games we play, both as adults and children, are a form of make-believe which not only enhances life but in some mysterious way offers us the key to true self-discovery. The West puts men on the Moon, the East puts men in touch with their real selves; or in other words, the animal within.

Clearly no one can foretell our destiny, and even if one could, so many conflicting factors would make escaping it an absolute impossibility. The Chinese Horoscope has little or nothing to do with the Western signs of the Zodiac. What it teaches is not a plan for tomorrow, but a way to know yourself today and every day. To learn who we are through our influencing animal is to take part in a wonderful ancient game that will make our lives both richer and happier.

Barry Fantoni's
Chinese Horoscopes

THE GOAT

1907	February 13th to February 1st	1908
1919	February 1st to February 19th	1920
1931	February 17th to February 5th	1932
1943	February 5th to January 24th	1944
1955	January 24th to February 11th	1956
1967	February 9th to January 29th	1968
1979	January 28th to February 15th	1980
1991	February 15th to February 3rd	1992

My men, like Satyrs grazing on the lawns,
Shall with their Goat feet dance the antic hay.

Christopher Marlowe

The Year of the Goat

The Goat's year will begin, continue and end on a note of total accord, for in the eyes of the Chinese, the Goat is seen as a harbinger of peace. Wars and international crises started in other years will find that their strength has been spent by the time they reach the Goat's year. Both personal and universal feuds will be resolved when faced with the Goat's power to calm and pacify as the countless examples testify. January 1919 saw the Peace Conference in Paris, and on June 19 of that year the Peace Treaty with Germany was signed at Versailles. In 1955 the World's leading scientists appealed for the renunciation of war because of the possible effects of the hydrogen bomb. In 1967 an International treaty was signed in Washington, banning nuclear weapons from outer space, the Moon, and other celestial bodies.

There will be plenty of scandal and gossip, however, and lots of squabbles. In May 1979 former Liberal leader Jeremy Thorpe went on trial at the Old Bailey, accused of conspiring to murder Norman Scott, his alleged lover. No big fights, to be sure – just a string of petty quarrels which are soon over and even sooner forgotten. But if there are no big punchers in the Goat's year it doesn't mean that sport gets left out in the cold. Although the Olympic Games are never held during the Year of the Goat, open any record book and you'll find it full of athletes who have excelled. The American miler, Jim Ryan, ran a world's best in 1967. In 1979 Seb Coe produced two magnificent performances: he set a new world record for both the 1,500 metres and knocked three seconds off Jim Ryan's fastest ever mile.

This is a splendid year for looking up old friends and visiting members of the family in far away places. It is, in fact, a good year for family life in general; a time to get married, have children and enjoy a little fun if it comes along. But don't go out of your way for it. It's a year to fill your home with beautiful objects and paintings; to line your shelves with your wine cellar with vintage clarets and the best port money can buy. In the year of the Goat there will be much wonderful music composed and played, and the theatre will see its finest actors and actresses performing in unforgettable productions. In 1955, the film *Rebel Without a Cause* introduced the world to James Dean, who added a new dimension to cinema acting. That same year the Vienna Opera House reopened, and the Soviet Union staged a performance of *Hamlet*, the first since the end of Tsarist Russia.

This is not the year to make plans or to design long term projects. Talk peace, but don't invest your life's savings in an industrial enterprise. Leave the stock market alone. Drink chilled wine in the long hot summer, eat lots of chocolate cake and gossip till dawn. The year of the Goat is one in which we should be guided by our instincts, and let them lead us to the Good Life.

The Goat is born under the sign of art
and loves all things beautiful

The Goat Personality

---

*'Time for peace and pleasure,
enter the charming and capricous Goat.'*

Of all the twelve signs of the Chinese horoscope, the Goat is the most uniquely feminine. Although universally respected for her shy and gentle manners, and her open sense of humour, the Goat is acclaimed above all as the Bringer of Peace. Nothing in the Goat's make up is hostile, and in so far as she shows aggression, it will only be as a means to restore harmony, peace and balance. But if you do bump into a Goat in a rage, you can be certain that her anger will be directed towards injustice. Wherever it is found, either in the wide and complex world at large, or in the confines of the home, the Goat is quick to react against conflict. For her, both the world and her home are of equal importance in matters of broken harmony, and nothing upsets her need for peace and contentment more than voices singing out of tune. As a kind of umpire, checking the Great Game we all play is played according to the rules, the Goat is at the heart of things. And no one loves to be at the centre more than a Goat; she takes to being the main attraction one might say, as ducks take to water. And there is no doubt that her love of the spotlight is the reason why the Goat makes such a fabulous hostess. No one puts on a more glittering show when entertaining. Only a Goat arranges her table with such artistry, has silver that gleams so bright and flowers that smell so sweet. And if you have some epicurean whim, there isn't a hostess on earth who will take greater care to ensure it is served exactly to your taste. If you want an omelette without eggs, you only have to ask the Goat hostess and it will be yours. And Mr Goat is no third-rate party giver either. For a classic example we need to look no further than the extravagances of the late Shah of Persia. Shortly before he was deposed, he spent billions building a city of gold in the middle of the desert and invited the world's most important, rich and influential people to share in what was estimated as the most expensive party ever thrown.

As well as his concern for plenty of bubbly and chin wagging with the in-crowd, the Goat has a highly developed artistic sense, and is born under the sign of art. Indeed the list of Goat celebrities include a high proportion of wonderfully talented, artistic people. If you were born in the year of the Goat, you share your sign with Herbert Von Karajan, Rudolph Valentino, George Harrison, Duke Ellington, Buster Keaton, Franz Liszt, Robert Graves, Marcel Proust and Andy Warhol.

Although the Goat has a great natural flair for any kind of artistic enterprise, whether it's perfecting the *pas de deux*, or baking a spinach soufflé, the Goat's genius is of the wayward variety. There are none of the heavy intellectual overtones as found in the Buffalo's creation, or the drama of the Tiger's artistry. The Goat's art is one of gentle reflection, and it is perhaps why the Goat expresses herself best when engaged in an artistic partnership, where another hand can act as a stabiliser and guide. The great composer Felix Mendelssohn enjoyed only a short life but wrote much music of lasting beauty. His father was an essential figure in Mendelssohn's career, treating him first as a son, and then as a kind of super-client, arranging his tours, publishers, holidays and just about everything else. And what of the Goat Mick Jagger? His song writing royalties have always been shared equally with Keith Richards (also a Goat), who many believe has helped Jagger more than anyone to keep the Stones rolling for so many years.

The Goat's ability to work easily with others is, I'm certain, the key to unlocking his temperament. Left to roam freely, the Goat will wander in your neighbour's field, and your neighbour's neighbour's field. Sometimes he'll eat everything in sight, including the old mattress and car tyres. The next day it will be your prize marrow. It is therefore in everyone's best interest, including the Goat's, that he be tethered. A rope around the Goat's neck removes their inbuilt craving for security, and in addition, leaves them free to enjoy their immediate surroundings in a way they would not normally do if left to their own devices.

The word 'enjoyment', of course is one placed very high on the Goat's list of most used words. And she has every right to enjoy her pleasure, for few can both give and receive with such good grace and charm. There are also few animals with quite such an extraordinary sense of humour, as the Goat Groucho Marx illustrates. But here, too, there is something of the Goat in need of a firm guiding hand. On the screen Groucho Marx was the hero of every plot, leading his hapless brothers in and out of a million wild and improbable scrapes. But in real life, Groucho was, according to his many biographers, a sad and lonely figure who was in desperate need of security right up to the very end. His romances and marriages collapsed more often than a clown's baggy trousers, and to this day there is still a dispute as to who is the rightful heir to his mammoth estate. And it might well be said that for every great Goat actor, you can bet your bottom dollar that there is strong support waiting in the wings. For every Laurence Oliver, there's a Vivien Leigh to give the performance that bit extra. Sir Larry is a classic Goat, and so is the dancer Anthony Dowell – a performer full of grace and subtle movement. And while on the subject of dancers, there are those who say the Goat Margot Fonteyn was never more nimble on her delightful feet than when Rudolph Nureyev (a Tiger) was by her side.

Because Goats tend to ponder a great deal before acting (or not bothering to act) they are very often poor decision makers and should not be left to make important decisions on their own. Fretful and whimsical, the Goat hates to commit himself, and will often wait for others to decide before acting. The trick, as the Goat sees it, is to let others do the worrying while they get on with life's big issue – having fun! This frequently has the effect of causing the Goat to become moody when the choice has been made against her wishes. But being a Goat, you'd never know you had made the wrong choice until it was too late. And when things go bad for a Goat, they really go bad. They are not good at coping with personal reversals, and are easily put off a project if the going begins to look tough. What is more, Goats cannot bear any kind of personal criticism. Tell a Goat that her lipstick is a tiny bit the wrong shade, or her watercress soup's on the thick side and you can cross yourself off her guest list! The Goat is far too polite to say anything there and then, but she won't forget. And while on the issue of guest lists, do not make the mistake of turning down a Goat's invitation, however casually it might appear to have been made. Rejection looms very large in the life of a Goat, and again exposes their basic sense of insecurity. A very noticeable characteristic of the Goat is his tendency to worry, almost fret, over trivialities.

Goats hate any form of restraint, and will fight shy of any role that imposes regularity and schedules. To be tethered to what a Goat finds agreeable is one thing, but to be harnessed to a routine is the Goat's idea of purgatory. Goats steer well clear of the Services, military or civil – unless of course, the job comes with a large house, servants and pots of money. And as a rule, Goats are best advised to avoid any form of commerce. In particular they should not apply for the job of salesman. They get easily flustered, and it is then that they might snap just a little. Remember, they have very sharp teeth, and a pair of back legs that can pack a hefty kick.

The really insecure Goat, the one who knows it, will need a great deal of support. To be thought well of causes such

Goats to introduce a false note in their behaviour; to have a pronounced social awareness. However much she puts into the preparation of food for a dinner party, even more care and attention will have gone into the composition of the guest list, which will contain as many fashionable and famous names as she can muster. And there in the centre of all these bright and witty people is the Goat herself, the very hub of it all. This in turn leads us to be cautious when the Goat gives 'us her seemingly well-informed opinion of the current theatrical hit, or some other fashionable event. Her intention will not be to inform us, but to create an impression, which leads us to ask if the opinion she expresses so confidently is her own or her favourite reviewer's? And when we look through her book-shelves, aren't all those books in the bestseller lists? And the new oil painting over the fireplace, her choice or the Bond Street dealer's?

In the Goat's home there will be no shortage of bric-a-brac. There'll be etchings, records, videos, knick-knacks, heirlooms, junk from the local shop, junk from Christie's, hallstands, mirrors, old chairs with the stuffing coming out, sofas from Harrod's, Victoriana, art nouveau, art deco, wall hangings, coffee tables, coffee table books, cats, dogs, hamsters and children – lots of them. No one is more acquisitive than the Goat, and it is a trait that runs through both male and female alike. No matter what the cost, or whether she really wants it, the Goat will take her momentary fancy home. The lady on the package tour with the sombrero, castanets, and plastic bag bulging with duty free is almost certain to have been born in the year of the Goat.

As the French author Paula Delsol tells us in her book *Chinese Horoscopes*, the Goat enjoys what the Japanese call I-Shoku-Ju, which, roughly translated, means the love of the senses: food, clothes and comfort. No wonder there are always a handful of slimming books in the Goat's bookcase. But a life centred on its superficialities, however agreeable, can only spell trouble when dealing with serious matters. It is here that the Goat shows herself at her most fickle. In matters of love, as with everything else, Goats do not know the meaning of self-denial. When in love with a Goat, you will want to know her true feelings. But because she never wants to be thought ill of, and has an in-built desire to preserve peace, the Goat will often back away from her real feelings. When you ask simply, 'Do you love me?' the Goat will invariably give you the answer she imagines you want to hear. The same might be true for her opinion of your latest sonnet, your new car or your holiday snaps. This kind of detached response is perfect for an actor, whose lines are fiction to begin with, but in everyday life it can lead to insurmountable problems. Lucky, then, that the Goat has a remarkable gift for getting out of tight spots; namely, her immense charm. And make no mistake, the Goat can really turn on the charm when she wants something. What is more, if it's a man the Goat is interested in, he will soon know it. By flirting, pouting, throwing moods, even throwing off her underwear, the lady Goat will get her man. Her only problem is whether she really wants to keep him. With the wayward and coquettish Goat, it's always difficult to tell.

When a Goat does settle down, her family completely dominates her life, and she'll devote every ounce of her considerable energy to making sure her husband and children are contented.

Not much will escape her maternal eye, and no child of a Goat mother will be sent to school with holes in his shoes or a dirty shirt collar. And her husband won't exactly leave home looking as if he'd spent the weekend swilling out the pigsty. But for all her concern about family appearances, the Goat mother will not become a housemaid. Husbands and children can do their own ironing and clean their own shoes. She'll be there at inspection time, making sure that everything is tickity-boo, but that's her last line of commitment. Self-help is the by-word in the Goat's home.

Although Goats tend to leave their homes while still young, they have a curious habit in later life of moving close to their parents. One Goat lady I know married, had two children, and lived close to my own home. As her children grew she decided a bigger house was needed and started looking around. With the whole of London to choose from, she moved one door away from her mother. Another Goat lady, who is a friend of my wife, goes to live in her mother's house every weekend. And my uncle Edward lived in his mother's house from the day he was born until the day he died, aged eighty-five.

In spite of the Goat's desire for security, plus the fact that she is impressionable and easily led, the Goat lady is very much the boss in her own home. Not the one to make the choice, the Goat will subtly influence all the important decisions. Somehow the choice of where the family Goat takes its holidays, the type of car, the school its children go to, all of these home-based decisions will ultimately require the final approval of the lady Goat. It is therefore imperative that the Goat marries someone who is both strong and adaptable. He most certainly will need a strong head for drink with all those late night parties.

Because Goat ladies are easily impressed, they in turn like to impress, and their clothes often mirror this attitude. Even the most conservative Goat lady will aim to wear the kind of outfit that will win not only the admiration of her own man, but everyone else's. No matter what they dress up in, whether it's a leather mini-skirt or a see-through blouse, the Goat lady will put her need to be noticed top of her list and the need to feel comfortable way down at the bottom. Goat men, on the other hand, dress very much to suit themselves. If they work in a job where they can wear what they like – and most Goats do – they'll go in for shabby old corduroys, heavy tweeds and colourful woollen neck-ties. You might well find a Goat in second-hand clothes – the well worn feel and quality appeals to the Goat, as do spotted handkerchiefs tied into a cravat, and open sandals when the weather's fine. And Goat men very often wear their clothes until they fall apart at the seams.

When choosing a profession, Goats should stick to the world of the arts, although if they do decide that they are mountain Goats, and care to climb Everest, they will be in good company. Sir Edmund Hillary was a Goat. But there are a few pitfalls facing the lady Goat, and her innocent love of *la dolce vita* could easily find her serving drinks to tired businessmen in a Soho club, if you get my drift. However, the Chinese believe that a Goat in the home brings good fortune as the Goat has a pure heart. This means that he will always have money, although he will not necessarily always be wise in the way he spends it. But once a Goat gets the hang of finance, he will exercise great shrewdness in his business dealings.

Goats have the justified reputation for surviving almost anywhere – from the sun parched deserts to the steepest mountains. Even so, I don't expect many Goats plan to climb

Mount Everest in their fortnight break, or cross the Gobi on a camel. Goats adore the Good Life and they only need the advice of a decent guidebook to help them make up their minds. Always going for the best they can afford, Goats will be discovered on the sun-drenched beaches of exotic locations like Thailand, and in the seafood restaurants of Normandy. Social and easy-going with strangers, Goats will go anywhere the food is good and the wine is drinkable. They will fill the nightclubs and their love of art will not exclude an evening at a concert of afternoon in the local museum.

The first of the Goat's three phases of life will find the young Goat clinging to the family, and she'll be one of those children who will be quick to use her tears to get her own way. But her fickle nature will lead her to want her own life and she'll leave home while still very young – coming back every time she gets into hot water. Driven by her senses, the Goat will suffer complications, especially in matters of love. But she is not foolish and quickly learns from her mistakes. Once the Goat realises that her own patch of ground is no greener than the patch on the other side of the fence, she will settle down to a long and contented final phase, and will be visited often by her large and loving family.

Goats adore good company

Goat as Parent

The mother Goat and her daughter kid will have an almost perfect understanding, as both are aware from a very early age just what trouble a capricious heart can get them into. There will be no moralising between them, nor will there be any great competition, just a regular session of exchanging notes. The Goat mother's view of the baby Pig will not be very different, and she'll encourage the social side of his character so that he learns to play as well as work. 'Thank you very much,' says the Pig in genuine gratitude. The Horse daughter will also grow up contentedly in a Goat's home; nice clothes, good school, riding lessons ... The baby Cat will also enjoy life with a Goat as a parent. He is an artistic child and the Goat father will do his best to encourage his talented son. But Kittens need a lot of pushing to get them off on the right foot.

The Goat father will adore his Monkey daughter, but she'll suffer from his over-indulgence in later life. Alas, we cannot trick our way out of every tight corner, not even if we are the cleverest of Monkeys. Snake children have a slight chance of happiness in the house of a Goat parent. They mature very slowly and the Goat mum insists her Snake daughter glitters at every social function – often put on for the daughter's benefit. Nevertheless, the Goat mother will support her Snake offspring, even though she might receive a small return for her investment.

On the other side of the coin, the Dragon son can do no wrong in the eyes of his Goat mother. The problem facing parent and child here is how to introduce some kind of critical appraisal. All that showing-off might get the Dragon somewhere in life, but what if it doesn't? The reverse is true for the young Buffalo. He's such a solitary child, and to get him to say anything to all the high-spirited guests the Goat brings home ... well! Young Tigers will be happy enough to say a few polite words to the Goat's friends, and even amuse them. Tiger children can be very cute. But they'll grow sick of the rich sponge cakes and lack of adventure.

The baby Rooster *thinks* she likes the Goat's somewhat shambolic home life, but great method burns within her young heart, and a sense of what is right and wrong is also deeply etched there. The Dog child will form a good relationship with the Goat parent. Son or daughter, the young Dog will love and be loved by the Goat, and the love will grow stronger as they all grow older. Dogs will visit their Goat parent in old age, and never reproach them for having low horizons. The young Rat can get nothing from a Goat parent but more of what he has already. He might like it, but it won't do the Rat child any good to throw his charm around. To be truly successful, the baby Rat must be given the kind of tools the Goat doesn't own.

Compatibility of Goat Parent and Child

Rat	☐
Buffalo	☐
Tiger	☐
Cat	😊😊😊
Dragon	😊😊😊😊
Snake	😊😊😊
Horse	😊😊😊😊
Goat	😊😊😊😊😊
Monkey	😊😊😊
Rooster	☐
Dog	😊😊
Pig	😊😊😊😊

Goat in Business

Goats, broadly speaking, are at their best when involved in some way with the arts, however tenuous the connection might be. It therefore follows that they should steer well clear of business, especially the industrial areas. A partnership of two Goats is not a good idea, as both need a strong hand to help produce their best. But an escort agency might work out all right. A steadying influence will be found under the practical and hard working Horse. The Goat and Horse are natural partners in many fields and the world of commerce is no exception. The honest Pig might not tether the Goat, but he will make sure that the work gets done, even if he has to do a bit extra himself.

If the Goat is an actor or an actress, or someone who works for a fee rather than a wage, he or she would be well advised to find themselves a Cat for an agent. They will sniff out the best jobs and ensure that the Goat gets the top price. The Dragon is a strong leader, and the Goat will be quite happy to follow the Dragon's great schemes. But if the Goat sits in the driver's seat he'll change direction too many times for the Dragon. The Goat's on/off attitude will exasperate the Dragon, who will sell his shares and move on.

The opportunist Rat sounds like a good bet to partner the Goat, but they both have a very different method of arriving at the same goal. Rats grab, Goats lay traps, and in business it does not pay to have a divided front. But Rat and Goat can make money – a firm of liquidators, perhaps, or auctioneers? The Tiger has plenty of schemes up his sleeve, but he'll want the kind of firm commitment and instant action that the Goat is seldom happy giving. The Monkey is good with money, and takes his time deciding on the best investment. This is good news for the indecisive Goat. But he must be careful how he deals with the profits the Monkey so carefully accrues. No wild spending. Spending the profits is a problem facing the Snake and Goat as partners. The only partnership for these two would be one financed by a trust, so the money would never be theirs to spend. Perhaps they should run the British Museum.

The resolute Buffalo knows how to get the Goat working, but the Goat has his own pace and his own very specific ideas about work and leisure being quite separate. Nothing but prolonged and bitter arguments here. There is no point in a Rooster teaming up with a Goat, even if they are good friends. The Rooster is well organised and thinks positively. Why can't the Goat stick to one thing at a time? The Dog is not cut out for the wheeler-dealer side of commerce, which is the only aspect a Goat can handle. No routines, just lots of deals. The Dog is the complete reverse. He'll be driven bonkers by the Goat's wayward approach, and be at the double vodkas to steady his nerves before you can say Jack Russell.

Compatibility of Goat in Business Relationships

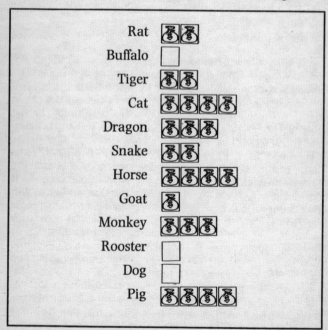

Goat in Love

Goats are no strangers to the complex affairs of the heart, and generally speaking don't have a great deal of control over them. This can obviously lead to all manner of complications, and in many ways hinders the Goat's, if you will pardon the expression, 'joy of sex'. For the partner who will give him least problems on the emotional front, the Goat might well fall in love with the sensuous Cat. She has a comfortable home and a very comfortable bed. But the Goat should at all times avoid animals with a highly developed sense of morality. The Rooster, in spite of his boasting, is deeply conservative in all matters concerning love, and will not go along with the Goat's capricious attitude. The anxious, loyal Dog won't care for it much, either.

The Buffalo shares the Rooster's strait-laced views on sex, but in this case that won't be his problem. When the Buffalo does actually manage to get the fires of passion burning, he'll have found to his dismay that the Goat has nibbled through her tether, and is in someone else's meadow. As for the Rat and Goat 'getting it all together', the chances are very slim indeed. They both prefer someone else's hayloft, and would never know where they were supposed to meet. There'll be no problems with the sexually easy Horse, and he'll charm and be charmed by the Goat. A perfect partnership so long as the Horse remembers not to use up all his stamina showing off in the five mile chase. Pigs are not complicated lovers, but come unstuck when they fall too heavily. The Goat might enjoy having a moon-eyed Pig at her elbow day and night. There again, she might not. The Tiger is hot blooded and passionate, and will be quickly taken in by the Goat's promises. But the Goat must be careful to keep them.

There will be no long term conclusion to the Snake and Goat, at least, no long term passion. The Snake's love is too mysterious for the fickle Goat, and has so many strings attached. The playful Monkey won't bother with strings, and the Goat might think that this suits her at first. But what happens when she dials the Monkey's number and finds there is no answer? The fiery Dragon will seduce the Goat in a twinkling and they will enjoy love uncomplicated by guilt, but both enjoy quantity as well as quality. Who will grow tired first? To have an affair, someone has to make the first step, unless, of course, both lovers are clairvoyant. This won't be the case when two Goats fall in love. It will be fine so long as one of them declares an interest.

Compatibility of Goat in Love

Rat	☐
Buffalo	☐
Tiger	♡♡♡
Cat	♡♡♡♡
Dragon	♡♡♡♡
Snake	♡
Horse	♡♡♡♡♡
Goat	♡
Monkey	♡♡♡
Rooster	☐
Dog	☐
Pig	♡♡

Goat in Marriage

Once a Goat decides to settle down, for however brief a time, she becomes the perfect home maker. The glass-fronted walnut cupboards will be full of beautiful china and the wine cellar will never be short of good wines. Goats have an instinct for the Good Life, and will quickly fall in with any spouse who will help provide it. The intelligent and industrious Horse knows all about Georgian candlesticks and has the energy and know-how to deal with the Goat's need for security. For a marriage to last, the Goat need look no further than the Horse. A good partnership, too, when the Goat marries the refined and equally socially conscious Cat. Both love a comfortable home and adore children. The Monkey might well walk down the aisle with the Goat. But they have very strong opinions, both of themselves and just about everything else. Silly to break up a marriage just because they can't decide which wallpaper to put in the downstairs loo. The lady Rooster might well decide that the pattern on the wallpaper is the most important thing in the world, and could even come to blows over it. Goats and Roosters are not a good idea when it comes to setting up home. Snakes, especially males, will find an ideal companionship with a lady Goat. But it will help the Goat if the Snake husband has a well paid job, and it will help both of them if they become Jehovah's Witnesses – they have such romantic inclinations . . .

A Goat marrying a Pig will not find his mind bothered by the way the home should look. The Pig will just get on with it, and it will be just the way the Goat likes it. A lady Goat might easily marry a Buffalo – after all, he's so strong and resolute. Both like children and secluded gardens to sit quietly in on hot summer days. But the Buffalo is a bit of a bore at party time. The Goat should avoid the Dog, who is a terrible pessimist, and his pessimism will only magnify the Goat's own deep rooted insecurity. The Tiger will cut a dash alongside his charming Goat wife. But Tigers crave adventure, and the Goat can hardly hold her soirées in a tent in the middle of the jungle. Rats are warm hearted, and love society. They will easily marry a Goat, and just as easily wander off. And that will mean both partners having fun on the side. The marriage of two Goats will only work if the pasture is filled with instant grass. Both take what's going and do not plan. But a big family might keep two Goats together – or drive them further apart. The Dragon has great ideas about himself, as a husband and anything else he turns his hands to. But in marrying the Goat he will only be making a mistake, for her as well as himself. Dragons make decisions. Goats avoid them.

Compatibility of Goat in Marriage

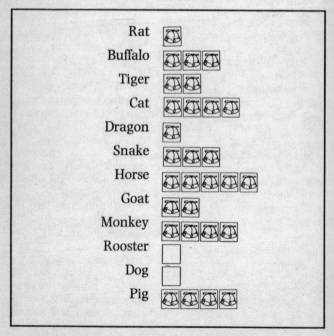

Anna Ford
(*Rex Features Ltd*)

Boris Becker
(*Popperfoto*)

Cecil Parkinson
(*City Syndication Ltd*)

Larry Hagman (*Rex
Features Ltd/Weber/Sipa Press*)

Ian Botham
(*BBC Hulton Picture Library*)

Margot Fonteyn
(*Rex Features Ltd*)

Cilla Black
(*City Syndication Ltd*)

Mick Jagger
(*Popperfoto*)

How you will be influenced in the Year of the Goat

A Year for Peace and Love

Bliss for the Goat! A mixed year for workers, but the shirkers do just dandy. The go-getting Rat can't believe his luck after the previous truly miserable twelve months. The Goat's year is a veritable cornucopia of delights for the opportunist everywhere, and the only problem facing the Rat is, will he eat too much? Careful fat Rat. The social Cat will be given ample opportunity to live life just how she wants under the influence of the equally socially inclined Goat. A fine year for Cats, but they must remember to get their beauty sleep.

The popular Horse will recover from his own year, should it have been a disaster (with the year of the Horse it is impossible to know). He'll get along well as long as he confines his practical skills to hanging paintings and opening the wine. And while there are plenty of parties, the merry Pig won't mind. He'll be there with his jokes and smiles and quickly-emptying glass. The Pig's one setback is in choosing which of the gilt-lined cards that decorate his mantelpiece he'll have to say 'sorry' to. The Monkey will take what's on offer – when doesn't he? And it will be fine until he realises he's the one who has to foot the bill.

There are two Roosters: the spendthrift type and those who save every penny. No matter which, they'll be footing *all* the bills in the Goat's year, and neither sort will do it graciously. The unpredictable Tiger will love everything that's going during the first few months, but as he begins to realise that it's all fun and games, he'll grow bored and restless. The subtle Snake will enjoy the flood of artistic achievements but will not find the sexual competition much fun. In fact, she'll loathe it. But sex wars never worry the dutiful and hard-working Buffalo. Nor does sex peace. He's simply not interested. Cocktail parties are neither for the Buffalo nor the loyal, idealist Dog, and both he and the Buffalo might as well move into a quiet corner and wait till the Goat's party guests start asking for their hats and coats.

The Dragon doesn't usually have a bad year, but when he does, this is it. The leader of the carnival goes around puffing fire and filling the air with his flames. The poor old Dragon; he glitters, he seduces, he stimulates, but no one pays him the least bit attention. Well ... maybe just one.

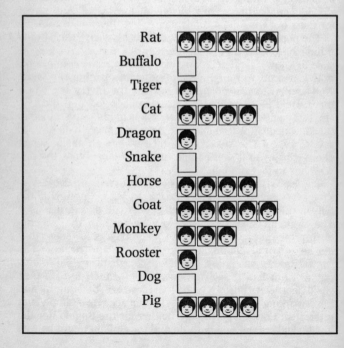

Famous Goats

Terence Conran

In Japan there is an expression which is a perfect summary of the Goat's personality; *I-Shoku-Ju*. Roughly, it means the love of the good life. Goats love everything that inspires the senses – classy cuisine, fine clothes and a beautiful home are all dear to a Goat's heart. It is therefore hardly surprising to find that the figure who has almost single-handedly shaped the taste of middle class Britain for nearly two decades was born in the Year of the Goat. It would have been surprising if he had not.

Terence Conran was born in Esher on October 10, 1931, the son of a gum importer. (One is tempted to add that it was a job that young Terry couldn't stick.) The Goat's waywardness expressed itself early. Young Terence was expelled from his school, Brystan, before entering art college to study textiles. Typical of the Goat, too, is the love of society. Examine any trendy group and you'll find a Goat at the centre. After art school, Terence enjoyed a kind of bohemian life style concentrated around Chelsea and the King's Road. His contemporaries were Mary Quant and Laura Ashley.

Goats are always concerned about what they put in their stomachs. Conran began making his pile, (his personal fortune is estimated at £100 million) from being the co-founder of a chain of soup kitchens back in the fifties. His style was evident from the start. His eating houses had pine tables and clean linen. The service was sound and the food cheap but good value. Above all, Conran's soup kitchens were trendy.

As a rule, Goats are not innovators. Their great strength is in their ability to recognise and reshape the qualities of others and their creations. Conran's whole success has been based on such a recognition. His approach to the revolution in our homes, in what we wear, what we eat and what we clothe our children in is the result of borrowing from those who are actually original. There are those who think of Conran as a designer; they are wrong. The head of Mothercare, Heals, Next, Richard Shops and BHS is an astute business man with an eye for well designed goods. In an uncharacteristic moment of honesty − Goats find telling the truth about themselves tough going − Conran once told a child, who has asked him what a plagiarist was, 'I am.' Even so, isn't there just a hint of self-satisfaction about Sir Terry's reply? Goats can be awfully full of themselves at times.

No Goat can resist a party, especially when they are to be the centre of attraction. Birthday parties suit the Goat down to the ground. The late Shah of Persia, a Goat, once spent billions to celebrate the birth of his country. When Conran hit the age of fifty, his guests drank vintage champagne, ate the best food money could buy and the evening ended with a bang − a huge firework display. But beauty lover to the last, Sir Terry was up the next morning, clearing away the mess himself. And it is worth mentioning that there's none of the Habitat/cheapo look *chez* Conran. His three homes could only be described as sumptuous.

Goats are not over-generous, although they will never admit it, or indeed understand the charge. Of course, not all Goats are tight, but those who make fortunes tend to hang on to them. Conran has been known to retrieve Letraset sheets from the waste-paper baskets in order to save the letters X and Z. And in keeping with the Goat's romantically capricious side, Britain's foremost trend setter has been married three times. He actually married his first wife, Shirley Conran (a Monkey) twice.

Someone once said of Terence Conran, rather unkindly that, 'He labours under the illusion that he is the only person ever to have got to France.' But Sir Terence is quite clear about his role. 'I am interested in getting things done.' he says. 'Changing the face of Britain has been my dream.' There are many who will say his dream has been well and truly realised.

Margot Fonteyn

Goats everywhere have a strong need to perform. For most, however, this need might be limited to something slightly less glamorous than the stage at Covent Garden. Throwing a dinner party requires a performance of sorts, and when a Goat is the host or hostess they will certainly give the evening everything they've got. They will dress to the nines, cook exquisitely and conduct the topics of conversation as if they were movements of a symphony. No matter what, the Goat will be the very centre of attention. But there are some Goats who have the good fortune to express their urge to perform through a more public route. Born under the sign of Art, Goats have nimble feet and in Greek mythology, Satyrs were depicted as Goat-like men who sang, drank and danced. They loved a knees up. One of the greatest dancers of all time was born in the Year of the Goat.

Born plain Peggy Hookham on May 18, 1919, Dame Margot Fonteyn was born in England, although she spent much of her childhood in China. No doubt it is the Goat's love of beauty that led Dame Margot to change her name. Can you see the neon lights – Rudolph Nureyev and Peggy Hookham in *Swan Lake?* No, neither can I.

Goats are above all a feminine sign, and ballet is the perfect means of expression for Goats with a performing instinct. True to her sign, Margot Fonteyn began to dance at a tender age. She took her first lessons shortly after her sixth birthday.

Another important feature of the Goat's personality is their gift of interpretation. Although not always original in their creativity, the Goat has few peers when it comes to handling the originality of others. Margot Fonteyn's career as a dancer has been greatly enhanced by having formed very important partnerships with two outstanding individuals.

The first was with Frederick Ashton, one of the most highly respected choreographers of all time. Born in 1904 – the year of the Dragon – Sir Frederick Ashton responded fully to his animal influence. His flair for the unorthodox productions of classical roles provided a superb vehicle for Margot Fonteyn's elegance. He said of her; 'Never once did she make a gesture which was not completely true, one that did not come from the heart.'

As great a ballerina as she was, it was only when Dame Margot met Nureyev that her dancing reached its full and glorious goal, the point at which she could be called, *prima ballerina absoluta*; the world's best!

Rudolph Nureyev was born on 17 March, 1938, the year of the Tiger. His dancing is a distillation of the Tiger's vigorous and vital nature. Ideas tumble out. With Nureyev at her side, Dame Margot danced with fire as well as grace. She added an inner passion to her roles which matched Nureyev's electric brilliance, and moved all those who saw it.

Because they need to be tethered, Goats are capable of being led anywhere. And there is nothing easier than leading a Goat astray. In 1967, Margot and Rudy were arrested for a drug offence at a party in San Francisco. But the charges were dropped once it was discovered who the couple were. Even so, Tiger and Goat had a few tricky hours before being released.

Having danced longer than most other ballerinas, Dame Margot has now more or less retired. Today she devotes her time to her husband, Dr Roberto de Arias. A Dragon, like Ashton, Dr de Arias was the victim of an assassination attempt in the sixties. It left him paralysed. Tethered to her crippled husband, Dame Margot Fonteyn continues to display the Goat's great artistic qualities in her home and her caring for Roberto. And as always is determined to give of her best.

Ian Botham

Because Goats are born under the sign of Art, it would be a serious mistake to think of them as soft. Quite the opposite is true. Goats excel in the performing arts, which require great stamina and dedication. And there are many performers who do not confine their skills to the concert platform or theatre. Today sport is considered by many to be little more than an extension of the performing arts. Commentators are frequently heard describing a dribble down the touch line as if it were something out of *Swan Lake*. And with good reason. Sportsmen and sportswomen are often extremely graceful. But of all sports, few get closer to pure drama than cricket. A five day test match can involve tragedy, comedy and sometimes farce. One player who embodies all three dramatic extremes, both on and off the field is the man some think of as the greatest all rounder ever.

Ian Botham was born on November 24, 1955, and carries all the trimmings of the male Goat. His designer clothes, bleached hair and £22,000 Jaguar all reflect the Goat's concern with trend. Goats can't bear the idea of being out of date, which they see as placing them at a serious social disadvantage. Goats love to be the centre of attention – they put themselves first, (although you'll never meet a Goat who will admit it).

It can't be said often enough that a Goat needs tethering to make the most of themselves. In some cases, this might simply mean clinging to a dream, or the realisation of an ambition. Boris Becker and Steve Ovett are both examples of Goats who have tethered themselves to ambition. But tennis and athletics are games for individuals. Cricket, on the other hand, is a team game. Individuals are important in a cricket match, but they must be able to put self interest second to the team's. The question is how does a player like Ian Botham, who loves the limelight, take a back seat when told to? The answer is simple; first find a cricket playing Horse. When examining the Chinese Horoscope, you will find few partnerships which are more auspicious.

Although Botham has already written himself into the pages of cricket history, his finest hour was under the England captain, Mike Brearley. Born on April 28, 1942, Brearley was born in a Horse year. As a captain he displayed all the Horse's great qualities – leadership, clear head, calmness under pressure. Under Mike Brearley, Ian Botham helped to bowl and bat England to an astonishing three wins on the trot against a tough Australian side. In one match, Botham scored a century off eighty-six balls. In the next Test, he took five wickets for one run. The next Test saw Botham hit another ton, this time off eighty-four balls. And on each occasion, Brearley the Horse was on hand to offer a few well chosen words of comfort and advice.

Luckily for Ian Botham, when he decides to go home, he

finds another Horse waiting to lay a soothing hoof on his weary shoulder. Botham's wife, Kathy, was born in 1954 and speaks with the Horse's fondness for not mincing words. She says of her cricket playing Goat; 'He's always here, there and everywhere. He was that way when I married him and he'll always be the same.'

Seldom out of the headlines, Ian Botham seems to have the knack of surviving the scandals he himself provokes. He also knows how to make money, another strong Goat characteristic. He earns over £300,000 a year, and his manager (another example of the tethered Goat) says that Ian has only seen the tip of the iceberg. It is estimated that before long Ian Botham, cricket's black Goat, will be the game's first millionaire. It is another record which few will begrudge him.

Mick Jagger & Keith Richards (both Goats)

Of all the twelve animal signs who make up the Chinese Horoscope, there are one or two pairings who, in spite of warnings against it, can't resist getting involved with each other. Two Goats have a very poor compatibility rating. They are advised not to marry, form business partnerships, or even fall in love. But because the Goat is so capricious, they frequently ignore such well-founded advice and seek each other out. And in the realm of the performing arts, there is evidence that two Goats might easily benefit from forming a partnership. In the case of the Rolling Stones, a couple of Goats have pretty well kept the show on the road.

Mick Jagger and Keith Richards were both born in the Year of the Goat – 1943. Mick was born on July 26, and Keith on December 18. Goats need tethering to make the most of themselves, and Mick and Keith are no exception. They met for the first time aged ten, at the Dartford Maypole County

Primary School, and have been tethered to each other ever since.

Almost nothing is more exhausting than a major rock band tour. When it's the most famous rock band in the world it's even tougher. What with groupies, hangers on, press officials, pushers and unending miles of motorway, no wonder the Stones got stoned. But Goats are hardy animals. They eat anything and sleep anywhere. Goats are capable of surviving in almost any conditions, and both Mick and Keith are survivors. They clearly turn to each other for inspiration.

Goats are born under the sign of Art and as a song writing team, Mick Jagger and Keith Richards have added immeasurably to the material now found in the Great Rock and Roll Song Book. Many of their titles alone have become verbal currency. 'Mother's Little Helper', 'It's All Over Now' and 'I Can't Get No Satisfaction', are all typical examples of Stonesspeak.

Royalties from the Jagger/Richards pen have put both Goats in the super millionaire league. But Goats are *so* capricious and there's no guarantee that once he has made his pile the Goat will hang on to it. In this respect, the song-writing Rolling Stones are like the wise and foolish virgins. Having studied at the London School of Economics, Mick Jagger's cautious approach to money (tight-fisted) is legendary. Often spotted on his way to Lords with an F.T. under his arm, Jagger's financial acumen would grace any city boardroom. Keith, on the other hand, is equally famous for his debts. Not surprisingly, he gives to all who ask, once donating £13,000 to sponsor Daley Thompson in the 1984 Olympics.

Not unlike a pair of mountain Goats, Mick and Keith have scaled the highest peaks. Of the two, Jagger has had the greater instinct for self preservation. When the gales blow, he keeps clinging on. Keith falls off. But Keith has always had the more interesting comments to make. He has been a more forthright interviewee. And typical of the Goat's personality, Keith Richards has a strong feeling for home and harmony; 'If you're going to have kids, look after them,' he once said. 'If you're going to dump the old lady, take care of her.'

Today, aged forty-four apiece, Mick and Keith continue to tour, write and record; they spend more time with their families than they do appearing before magistrates. To be Mick Jagger and Keith Richards demands an iron constitution – the constitution perhaps, that only the Goat can provide.

⛤⛤⛤⛤⛤⛤⛤⛤⛤⛤⛤⛤⛤⛤⛤⛤⛤⛤⛤⛤⛤⛤⛤⛤⛤⛤⛤⛤⛤⛤⛤⛤⛤⛤⛤⛤⛤⛤⛤

Goats pay a lot of attention to their homes and maintain strong family ties

⛤⛤

Famous Goats

Media
Dame Peggy Ashcroft
Jill Bennett
Buzby Berkeley
Leslie Caron
Diana Dors
Anna Ford
George Harrison
Mick Jagger
Buster Keaton
Ben Kingsley
Virginia McKenna
Frank Muir
Robert de Niro
Laurence Olivier
Buddy Rich
Keith Richards
Rudolph Valentino
John Wayne

Sports
Arthur Ashe
Boris Becker
Ian Botham
Mark Cox
Sir Edmund Hillary
Billie Jean King
Vicktor Korchnoi

Steve Ovett

Politics
Lord Carrington
Benito Mussolini
Cecil Parkinson
Norman Tebbit
Lech Walesa

Arts
W. H. Auden
John le Carré
Margot Fonteyn
Robert Graves
Oscar Hammerstein
Franz Kafka
Franz Liszt
Iris Murdoch
Frederick Raphael
Andy Warhol

Royalty
Shah of Persia

Others
Terence Conran
Marcel Proust

A Special Word on Compatibility

Throughout this book I have done my best to translate the Chinese view of compatibility with that of our own. But there are distinct differences between our two cultures which need clarification.

For the Chinese, love is seldom seen as something separate from marriage, an experience to be enjoyed in isolation. It is seen as part of a natural progression. In other words, love and marriage are thought of as a whole, and in this context their system of grading the compatibility of animal signs makes a lot of sense. In the West, if we have a love affair, we do so aware that it might or might not work out. In China that is not the case; there a couple find love later, accepting marriage as a kind of business relationship which is impossible to dissolve, no matter what. In China, it is imperative, therefore, that a Dragon, say, should marry a Rat, Rooster or Monkey; a Horse should marry a Goat, and a Dog should marry a Tiger.

But whatever your choice, the compatibility charts should not be read like the Ten Commandments, and not taken as law. They are more akin to a 'Good Food Guide'. We often enjoy meals in places with no stars, and are disappointed by five-star restaurants. It is the same with compatibility. If your partner is zero rated, but you love them, that's fine.

What the charts do, however, is prepare you for the future. Few people know what to expect when they embark on a new relationship. The changes that take place when a relationship develops badly are those we have all experienced; a sense of surprise followed by a sense of frustration. 'If only I had known this or that about him, or her', is a more than familiar expression, one we have almost certainly used ourselves. Quite simply, the job of the compatibility charts is to take the sting out of such a process. To be warned is to be prepared.

Above all, the compatibility charts provide a choice, saying if you want a relationship that is tailor made then here are the candidates. And if you want to put your money on an outsider, then it's up to you. But in any event, it must be emphasised that the compatibility charts are not carved in stone. At the same time, it is also worth remembering that they have been in existence for thousands of years. That they have stood the test of time, is, I believe, a tribute to their effectiveness.

Famous Goat Pairs, Couples and Groups

Heart and Rodgers   (both Tigers)
Frank Muir and Denis Norden   (Dog)
Margot Fonteyn and Nureyev   (Tiger)
Laurence Olivier and Vivien Leigh   (Buffalo)
Mick Jagger and Keith Richards   (both Goats)
Groucho Marx and Harpo   (Rat)
                    Chico   (Pig)
                    Zeppo   (Buffalo)

Find Your Partner's and Friends' Animal Signs

The Rat

1900	January 31st to February 18th	1901
1912	February 18th to February 5th	1913
1924	February 5th to January 23rd	1925
1936	January 24th to February 10th	1937
1948	February 10th to January 28th	1949
1960	January 28th to February 14th	1961
1972	January 15th to February 2nd	1973
1984	February 2nd to February 19th	1985

The Buffalo

1901	February 19th to February 7th	1902
1913	February 6th to January 25th	1914
1925	January 24th to February 12th	1926
1937	February 11th to January 30th	1938
1949	January 29th to February 16th	1950
1961	February 15th to February 4th	1962
1973	February 3rd to January 22nd	1974
1985	February 20th to February 8th	1986

The Tiger

1902	February 8th	to	January 28th	1903
1914	January 26th	to	February 13th	1915
1926	February 13th	to	February 1st	1927
1938	January 31st	to	February 18th	1939
1950	February 17th	to	February 5th	1951
1962	February 5th	to	January 24th	1963
1974	January 23rd	to	February 10th	1975
1986	February 9th	to	January 28th	1987

The Cat

1903	January 29th	to	February 15th	1904
1915	February 14th	to	February 2nd	1916
1927	February 2nd	to	January 22nd	1928
1939	February 19th	to	February 7th	1940
1951	February 6th	to	January 26th	1952
1963	January 25th	to	February 12th	1964
1975	February 11th	to	January 30th	1976
1987	January 29th	to	February 16th	1988

The Dragon

1904	February 16th	to	February 3rd	1905
1916	February 3rd	to	January 22nd	1917
1928	January 23rd	to	February 9th	1929
1940	February 8th	to	January 26th	1941
1952	January 27th	to	February 13th	1953
1964	February 13th	to	February 1st	1965
1976	January 31st	to	February 17th	1977
1988	February 17th	to	February 5th	1989

The Snake

1905	February 4th	to	January 24th	1906
1917	January 23rd	to	February 10th	1918
1929	February 10th	to	January 29th	1930
1941	January 27th	to	February 14th	1942
1953	February 14th	to	February 2nd	1954
1965	February 2nd	to	January 20th	1966
1977	February 18th	to	February 6th	1978
1989	February 6th	to	January 26th	1990

The Horse

1906	January 25th to February 12th	1907
1918	February 11th to January 31st	1919
1930	January 30th to February 16th	1931
1942	February 15th to February 4th	1943
1954	February 3rd to January 23rd	1955
1966	January 21st to February 8th	1967
1978	February 7th to January 27th	1979

The Monkey

1908	February 2nd to January 21st	1909
1920	February 20th to February 7th	1921
1932	February 6th to January 25th	1933
1944	January 25th to February 12th	1945
1956	February 12th to January 30th	1957
1968	January 30th to February 16th	1969
1980	February 16th to February 4th	1981

The Rooster

1909	January 22nd to February 9th	1910
1921	February 8th to January 27th	1922
1933	January 26th to February 13th	1934
1945	February 13th to February 1st	1946
1957	January 31st to February 17th	1958
1969	February 17th to February 5th	1970
1981	February 5th to January 24th	1982

The Dog

1910	February 10th to January 29th	1911
1922	January 28th to February 15th	1923
1934	February 14th to February 3rd	1935
1946	February 2nd to January 21st	1947
1958	February 18th to February 7th	1959
1970	February 6th to January 26th	1971
1982	January 25th to February 12th	1983

The Pig

1911	January 30th to February 17th	1912
1923	February 16th to February 4th	1924
1935	February 4th to January 23rd	1936
1947	January 22nd to February 9th	1948
1959	February 8th to January 27th	1960
1971	January 27th to February 14th	1972
1983	February 13th to February 1st	1984

A Brief look at the other Animal Signs

The Rat

The Rat is born under the sign of charm. Rats are warm, passionate and the supreme opportunist. They live for the day and seldom plan for tomorrow. Time does not concern them. Rats have sharp wits and an eye for detail, which favours them if they choose to become writers. Rats make excellent critics and salesmen. However, Rats have an undercurrent of aggression which occasionally expresses itself in worrying over details. In extreme cases, some Rats undergo a complete reversal and become obsessed by making plans and keeping statistics. Such Rats should not be rubbed up the wrong way. All Rats are devoted and love their family. They care little about their surroundings and are uncomplicated in affairs of the heart. Rats make money, but they cannot hold on to it. Rats love to scheme. They have a tendency to grumble when things go wrong.

The Buffalo

The Buffalo is born under the twin signs of equilibrium and tenacity. Buffalo people are conservative with a big and small

C, even if they hide behind a façade of being Left Wing. They work exceptionally hard and are strong and resolute in their business dealings. As parents they are firm and authoritative. Buffaloes are great achievers and feature prominently on the World Stage. They do not suffer fools, but find self criticism difficult. Buffaloes are stubborn and reliable, but they have complex hearts. In matters of romance they are often all at sea, seldom building lasting relationships. When a Buffalo has a conviction, he makes it the centrepiece of his life. Without conviction, a Buffalo can easily go to seed. Buffaloes do not care to share power. They love tradition and gardening.

The Tiger

Tigers are born under the sign of courage. They are brave, powerful people with a strong sense of their personal identity. They are natural revolutionaries and are disrespectful of authority. Tigers are quick tempered, and will risk everything for any cause that they believe in. This is particularly true of a Tiger in love. Tigers are great on ideas, seeming to possess a never-ending stream of original schemes. But the Tiger is a short paced creature and after a fast start, they are likely to run out of breath. They love to be the boss figure, usually ending up in charge of a team. The Tiger's life is often full of danger, and Tigers live life to the full. This sometimes means that a Tiger will meet a tragic and sudden end. Most of all, a Tiger needs to become fully himself, no matter what the cost. In other words, a Tiger needs to show the world what they are made of. They are very generous.

The Cat

Cats are born under the sign of virtue. They are social and refined with a good nose for bargains. Cats have good manners, good taste and place a high premium on family life. They are methodical, sometimes obsessively so. Cats are extremely diplomatic and are good listeners. Not original, Cats nevertheless show a great appreciation of beauty. They have shrewd artistic judgement and are acquisitive. Once a Cat has struck a deal he will keep it, come what may. Some Cats become ruthless when given power beyond their capability, but they are not normally concerned with matters outside domestic life. Cats hate change in routine and are sometimes a bit snobbish. Cats respond poorly to pressure, and will cave in emotionally under stress. A Cat's advice is well intentioned. They take their time when coming to a decision, and are very sensuous. All Cats dress well.

The Dragon

Dragons are born under the sign of luck. They are the national symbol of China and are believed to bring the three great eastern benedictions: wealth, long life and harmony. Dragons often become national heroes and have a magnetic personality. They are loved by many, but seldom love deeply in return. Dragons are impulsive, hot-headed and strive relentlessly for perfection. They have big hearts, broad interests and their advice is very wise. Dragons offer both their wisdom and professions of love freely and often. Dragons are generous, but often let their hearts rule their heads. Once they have begun a task, they see it through, regardless of its merit. Forced into a corner, the Dragon makes a poor judge and an even worse diplomat. They hate routine. Full of self-confidence, the Dragon can achieve anything.

The Snake

Snakes are born under the sign of wisdom. Guided by intuition, Snakes are wise, intelligent and think deeply. Snakes have a restless intellect which causes them to change direction many times in life. Although they do not give up easily, Snakes go through long periods of inactivity. This usually happens before a major change. Snakes are poor gamblers, and when asked to decide quickly, often make the wrong decision. They are possessive in human relationships and cling to those they love. Snakes are both peaceful and artistic, and have the gifts of music and humour. They are also capable of great artistic innovation. Snake women have the power to bewitch. Unlucky in love, Snakes can make a lot of money when they need to, and can become extremely wealthy. Snakes don't give up.

The Horse

The Horse is born under the twin signs of elegance and ardour. Horses are industrious and display a marked independence in everything they do. All Horses have great personality, which they trade on. They take naturally to any job that gives them freedom and a chance to exercise their great stamina. However, Horses become quickly bored and constantly take up new interests. When in love, the Horse becomes weak and unsure of himself. To make matters worse, Horses fall in love very easily. Although normally even tempered, the Horse can be provoked to terrible rages. Something of an egoist, the Horse can lead any crowd. He does not suffer fools and seldom gives an opinion without careful consideration. Horse women are witty and sociable.

The Monkey

Monkeys are born under the sign of fantasy. They are highly intelligent, active, and capable of turning their abundant skills to any use they choose. Above all, the Monkey has the power to win others over to his way of thinking. This they do by a mixture of art and craft. Talkative, humorous, with agile if somewhat imitative minds, Monkeys have a thirst for knowledge and new experiences. But Monkeys have a rather high opinion of themselves, and they are often superficial in their judgement of others. Monkeys are first class wheeler-dealers. They are careful with money, and it happens that they always make plenty. Monkeys are acquisitive and have wonderful memories. They are excellent organisers, but are easily seduced in affairs of the heart. Long-term relationships often elude the Monkey. In spite of the fact that Monkeys have few scruples, they care a great deal about their children. Monkeys will try anything once.

The Rooster

The Rooster is born under the sign of candour. They speak their minds frankly and openly, and always truthfully. They are deeply conservative, orderly in their daily lives, but have a boastful manner. Never short of an opinion, Roosters are sociable and spend much of their time dreaming up schemes which seldom bear fruit. In matters of finance, Roosters are either thrifty or spendthrifts; nothing in between. They are keen gardeners and adore home life. Successful in business, Roosters love the limelight, but they lack initiative and are best in partnership. Although they like to dress up and put on a show, Roosters are old fashioned in affairs of the heart. Roosters are honest, talkative and incorruptible. They regard their love life as strictly private and hold moral views on all matters. Roosters born between the hours of 5 and 7 are the most vocal. Lacking tact, Roosters are models of generosity. All Roosters are methodical.

The Dog

Dogs are born under the sign of loyalty. All Dogs are faithful, with warm hearts and a touchingly honest approach to everything they do. Dogs frequently find themselves defending those less fortunate and are just in their judgements. They fight bravely when roused, but have a tendency to act stubbornly. Dogs are practical in business but dither in the face of romance. Once set a worthwhile task, a Dog will never give up. They are watchful and often argumentative. The Dog's big problem is his constant anxiety. All Dogs suffer from an inability to stop worrying over details. They are occasionally blunt in their public dealings, but are easy going and delightful when in the company of friends. Dogs are good to their parents and never hypocritical. If he can tell the wood from the trees, a Dog will be a success. Dogs who have suffered bad experiences should be avoided. Dog women are often very vivacious.

The Pig
The Pig is born under the sign of honesty. Pigs are hard working and fun loving. Pigs enjoy all forms of social life and throw themselves into both work and leisure with great gusto. Big hearted, Pigs are jovial and forthright. They are lucky in business and seem to be able to make money whenever they want. In the matters of romance, Pigs are straightforward and direct; they are not ones for sophisticated courtship. Well informed and robust in character, the Pig is dependable and organises his life to suit himself. Sometimes the Pig has too high an opinion of his worth. Here he can be duped in his financial affairs or jilted in romance. Pigs adore their family and are generous with invitations to their homes. Slow to anger, Pigs are sometimes too gossipy for their own good. Men Pigs are often fancy dressers. Pigs are best in partnerships.

Author's Note

The Year of the Cat

Is it the year of the Cat, Rabbit or Hare? On the surface it is all a bit confusing, but there is a very simple explanation. The name you adopt depends very largely on which part of the world you come from. This is how it works.

Although it is true to say that the Chinese invented their wonderful horoscope, they are not the only ones who use it. During the 2,000 years it has been in existence the Chinese Horoscope has now travelled around the world. But if the horoscopes are new to us in the West, they have been with the nations close to China since the very start – well, almost. Not unnaturally each new country refined the twelve animal signs of the horoscope to suit themselves, to fit in with their particular culture. For instance, the people of Hong Kong name what the Chinese call the Rabbit, the Hare. In Vietnam, Cambodia and Korea, the Rabbit is called the Cat. The reason is simple. These people consider the word 'Rabbit' an insult. Likewise, many Chinese are offended at being termed a Cat.

My own researches show that the very first written word for the Cat/Rabbit/Hare year was, in Chinese, a 'creature with soft fur and a weak back'. Clearly it is a description which can easily fit all three animals.

Curiously the West did not learn about the Chinese Horoscopes from the Chinese, but from the Vietnamese who settled in France following the Indochinese war in the 50s. This is why so many Westerners call the years 1903, 1915, 1927, 1939, 1951, 1963, 1975 and 1987 the Year of the Cat.

But the most important point of all is to remember that all the experts agree that no matter what the word – Cat, Rabbit or Hare, the influence is *exactly the same*!

Also, the Rooster is sometimes called the Cock, the Buffalo the Ox, the Goat the Sheep and the Pig the Boar.

The author is grateful to the following reference sources for additional material:

Chinese Horoscopes by Paula Delsol, (Pan)
The Way to Chinese Astrology: the Four Pillars of Wisdom
Jean-Michel Huon de Kermadec, (Unwin)
The Handbook of Chinese Horoscopes Theodora Lau, (Arrow).

A selection of bestsellers from Sphere

FICTION

WANDERLUST	Danielle Steel	£3.50 ☐
LADY OF HAY	Barbara Erskine	£3.95 ☐
BIRTHRIGHT	Joseph Amiel	£3.50 ☐
THE SECRETS OF HARRY BRIGHT	Joseph Wambaugh	£2.95 ☐
CYCLOPS	Clive Cussler	£3.50 ☐

FILM AND TV TIE-IN

INTIMATE CONTACT	Jacqueline Osborne	£2.50 ☐
BEST OF BRITISH	Maurice Sellar	£8.95 ☐
SEX WITH PAULA YATES	Paula Yates	£2.95 ☐
RAW DEAL	Walter Wager	£2.50 ☐

NON-FICTION

AS TIME GOES BY: THE LIFE OF INGRID BERGMAN	Laurence Leamer	£3.95 ☐
BOTHAM	Don Mosey	£3.50 ☐
SOLDIERS	John Keegan & Richard Holmes	£5.95 ☐
URI GELLER'S FORTUNE SECRETS	Uri Geller	£2.50 ☐
A TASTE OF LIFE	Julie Stafford	£3.50 ☐

All Sphere books are available at your local bookshop or newsagent, or can be ordered direct from the publisher. Just tick the titles you want and fill in the form below.

Name _____

Address _____

_____

Write to Sphere Books, Cash Sales Department, P.O. Box 11, Falmouth, Cornwall TR10 9EN

Please enclose a cheque or postal order to the value of the cover price plus:

UK: 60p for the first book, 25p for the second book and 15p for each additional book ordered to a maximum charge of £1.90.

OVERSEAS & EIRE: £1.25 for the first book, 75p for the second book and 28p for each subsequent title ordered.

BFPO: 60p for the first book, 25p for the second book plus 15p per copy for the next 7 books, thereafter 9p per book.

Sphere Books reserve the right to show new retail prices on covers which may differ from those previously advertised in the text elsewhere, and to increase postal rates in accordance with the P.O.